CONTENTS

Drawing and Inking Tips

In the world of sword-and-sorcery, heroes can perform extraordinary feats of valour that would be impossible in the real world. However, it's still essential that your characters should look solid and believable. So here are some helpful hints to bear in mind.

1 First work out your hero's posture and attitude, using a wire frame. You can look in the mirror to establish how a pose might appear!

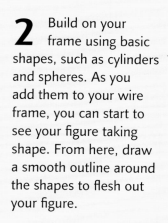

2 Build on your frame using basic shapes, such as cylinders and spheres. As you add them to your wire frame, you can start to see your figure taking shape. From here, draw a smooth outline around the shapes to flesh out your figure.

TOP TIP !

Most adult human figures are seven times the height of their head. Draw your character's head, then calculate his or her height by measuring three heads for the legs, one for the lower torso and two for the upper body.

HUMAN HEIGHT = 7 HEADS

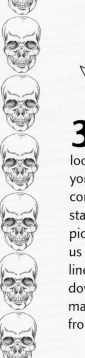

3 When things are looking good, and your character is complete, you can start to ink the picture. Inking allows us to choose the best lines we have put down in pencil, and make them stand out from the rest.

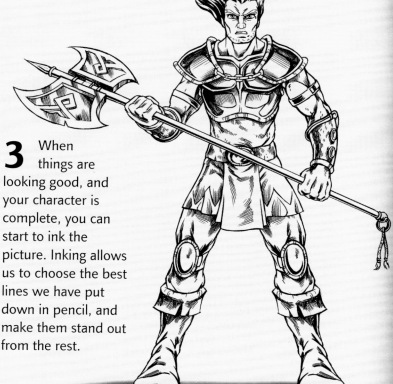

Colouring Tips

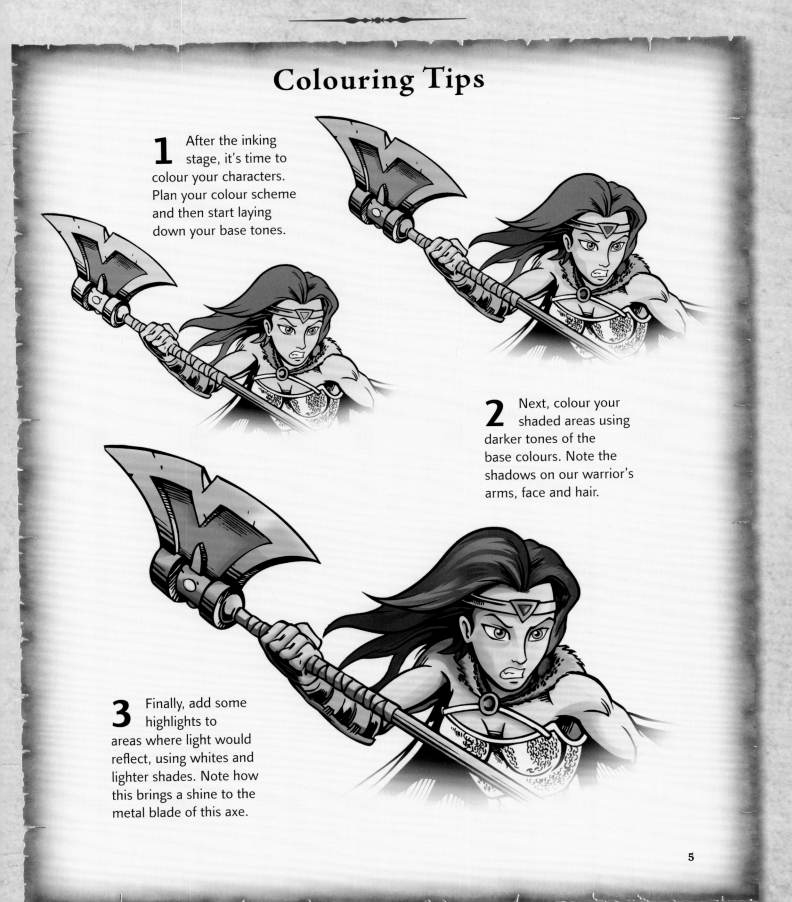

1 After the inking stage, it's time to colour your characters. Plan your colour scheme and then start laying down your base tones.

2 Next, colour your shaded areas using darker tones of the base colours. Note the shadows on our warrior's arms, face and hair.

3 Finally, add some highlights to areas where light would reflect, using whites and lighter shades. Note how this brings a shine to the metal blade of this axe.

5

MALE WARRIOR

This highly trained warrior is a fearless protector of the lands of light, who fights with unrivalled fury to uphold all that is good. All weapons are deadly in his hands and all opponents shall fall at his feet.

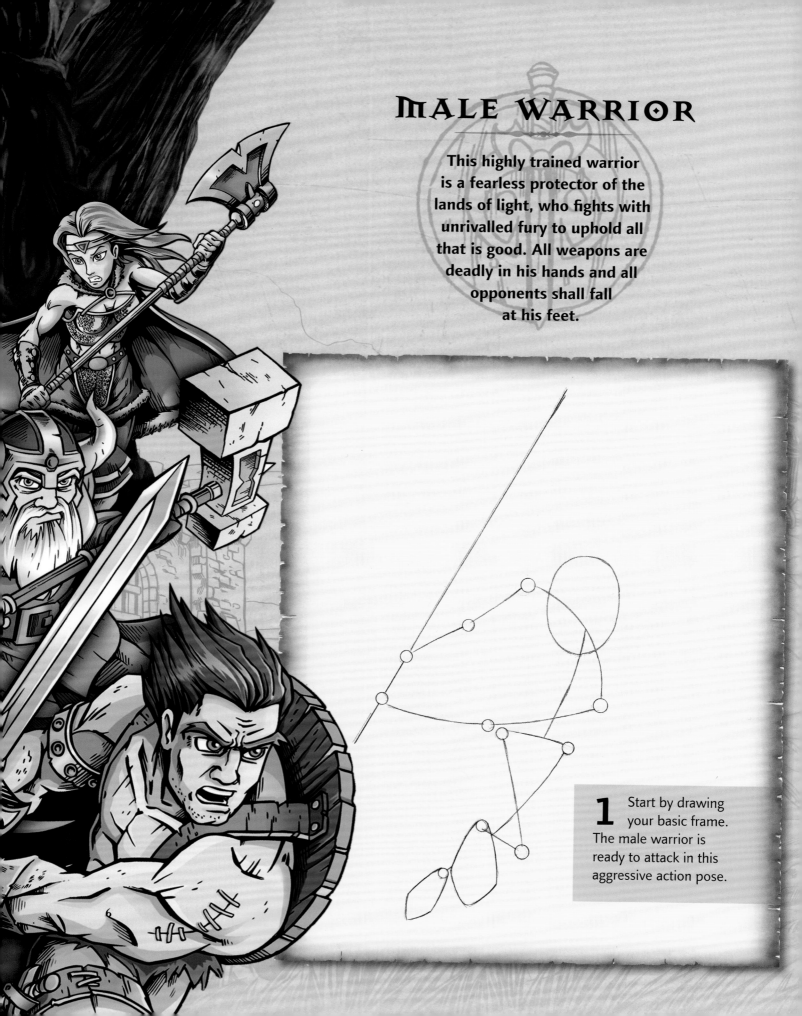

1 Start by drawing your basic frame. The male warrior is ready to attack in this aggressive action pose.

2 Warriors are tough fighting machines with broad shoulders and legs, so build on your wire frame with some hefty blocks as a base for all those muscles.

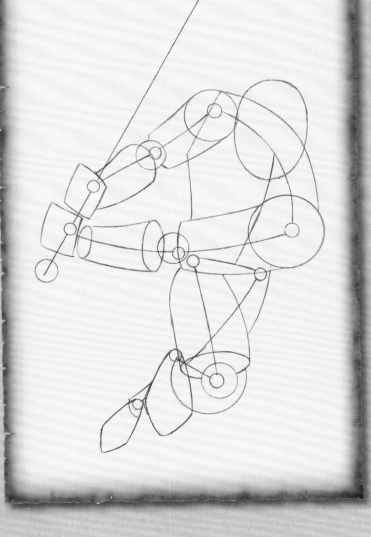

3 Once you have all of your basic shapes in place, draw around them to give your figure a smooth outline. At this point you can erase your wire frame. Pencil in your warrior's hair and the shape of his sword.

7

4 When you're happy with the outline of your figure, erase all of your basic shapes so that you have a clean pencil drawing. Now you can start adding detail. Mark in your warrior's clothing, leather wrist cuffs, shield and dagger. Give him a determined battle-ready expression, furrowed brow and an open, yelling mouth that will strike fear into the hearts of all who stand in his way!

7 The final step is to colour your warrior. Try to use shades that will enhance the different textures in the image. Use a bright yellow-gold for his metal sword, and muted browns for his wooden shield and leather boots. Use white to highlight where the light shines on his shield and the areas where it hits his body.

FEMALE WARRIOR

Loyal to her king, this agile fighter charges into battle with the ferocity and heart of a warrior twice her size, fighting for the forces of good. Many have mistakenly judged her by her size, and many have not lived to do so again.

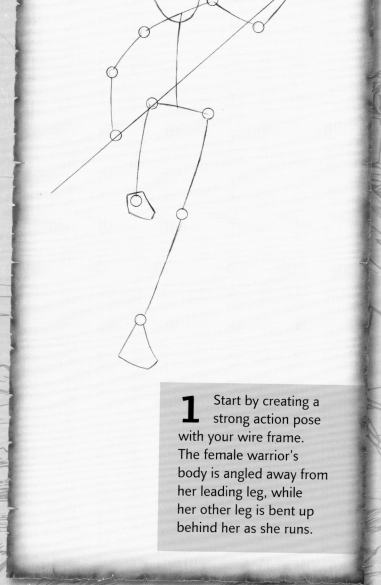

1 Start by creating a strong action pose with your wire frame. The female warrior's body is angled away from her leading leg, while her other leg is bent up behind her as she runs.

FEMALE WARRIOR

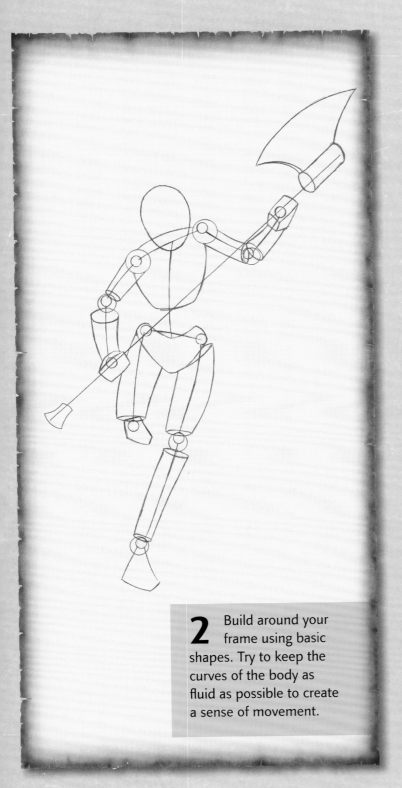

3 Once you can see your figure taking shape, erase your wire frame and draw around the shapes to create your outline. Start to add her clothing and hair.

2 Build around your frame using basic shapes. Try to keep the curves of the body as fluid as possible to create a sense of movement.

4 Erase all of your basic shapes so that you're left with a clean pencil outline, then start adding detail. Give her some body armour and finalise her clothing, adding a cloak and boots. Give her expression as much attitude as you would for a male warrior, but draw almond-shaped eyes, a smaller nose, and hopefully less stubble!

7 Now it's time to colour your character. Keeping your colour palette simple, then adding flashes of bright colours can be very effective. Shades of grey work well for her armour and weapon. Remember to add highlights to give the metal a reflective quality.

DWARF WARRIOR

From the stone kingdom of
the Western Mountains comes
this mighty warrior. Armed
with incredible strength and
determination, this dwarf likes
nothing more than seeing evil
fall beneath the power of his
ancient hammer.

1 Start by drawing
the basic stick
figure. The dwarf
warrior's body is short
and stocky, and he is
ready for battle.

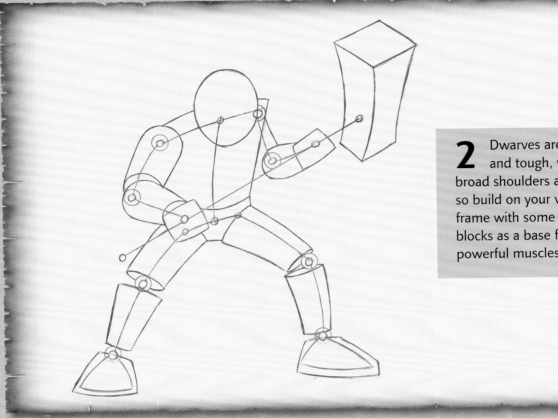

2 Dwarves are sturdy and tough, with broad shoulders and legs, so build on your wire frame with some hefty blocks as a base for those powerful muscles.

3 Keep building on your figure, removing your stick figure lines as it takes shape. The dome of his head will form the basis for his helmet. Add the horns on either side. Mark in his beard, clothing, boots and armour. Flesh out his hands and arms, and use blocks to divide his hammer's head into sections.

4 Finalise your pencil drawing, erasing your construction shapes as you go along. You now have the basis of a pretty dangerous warrior. Start adding the finishing touches like all the creases in his clothing and the detail on his helmet. Give him a determined, battle-ready expression.

5 Clean up the lines you have drawn and then add in all your final detail and shading. This will really bring your dwarf warrior to life.

TOP TIP !

Small details, such as chips and cracks, will help to make a weapon look old and battle-hardened.

6 Now you have everything in place, it's time to ink over your final pencil lines. Try to keep lots of the fine detail, like the chips and battle damage to his weapon and plates of armour.

7 The final step is to colour your warrior, which will really bring him to life. He is a brave and strong character, so rich colours will add a sense of heroism to his outfit. Give him a white beard and don't forget to add highlights to the metal of his armour.

Creating a Scene

THE BATTLEFIELD

Now that you've mastered how to draw three different types of characters, it's time to create a setting in which our heroes can appear. So welcome to the scene outside Blood Keep, a fortress which our valiant champions must protect at all costs.

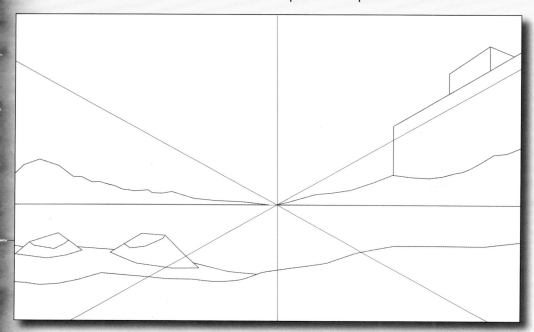

1 In this scene we have a central vanishing point, with perspective lines radiating from it. Elements such as the castle walls will follow the perspective lines until they hit that spot. Use the lines to plot out the basic shapes of the landscape and castle.

2 Next, add some extra elements and foreground detail, concentrating on simple shapes. Sketch out some pennants and battlements for the fortress; banners and weapons of fallen warriors on the battlefield; and some sinister skulls. You can put in as many elements as you like, depending on how busy you want your scene to be.

3 Flesh out your picture with more details, such as the tattered edges on the war banner and eye sockets in the skulls. Don't worry, you don't need to draw in every blade of grass! Concentrate on a few areas including the foreground, and it will give the impression that the entire area is grass-covered.

4 Your completed pencil drawing should look something like this. Finish off by adding fine details, such as the texture of the rocks, skulls and wooden poles, and the brickwork of the castle. Think about where shadows would be cast, and add shading. Remember to clean up any unwanted lines.

25

5 Now add some ink to your image. Remember to use dark, heavy inking in the foreground, and finer, lighter lines as objects get further away. This will help to give the image depth.

6 The colours you choose for your scene will dictate its atmosphere. Dark, night-time colours will create a sense of foreboding, while bright, daytime colours will create a sense of hope and optimism. A colourful sunset or sunrise – like the one shown here – suggests that things are about to change. But will they change for better or worse?

Movement and Combat

Once you are more confident with the basic construction of human-like characters, you can start experimenting with the way figures move. Try putting them in different action poses with different props and weapons.

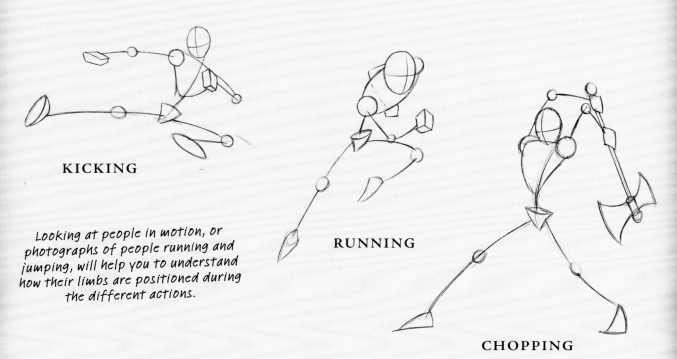

KICKING

Looking at people in motion, or photographs of people running and jumping, will help you to understand how their limbs are positioned during the different actions.

RUNNING

CHOPPING

Drawing two characters fighting isn't as hard as it might seem at first.
Follow the same steps that you would to create one character, but do it with two!

1 Draw the basic frame of one character first, and then the frame of his or her opponent. Build on the frames using your basic shapes, remembering how perspective will work on your characters, and that their sizes might differ depending on what sort of creature they are.

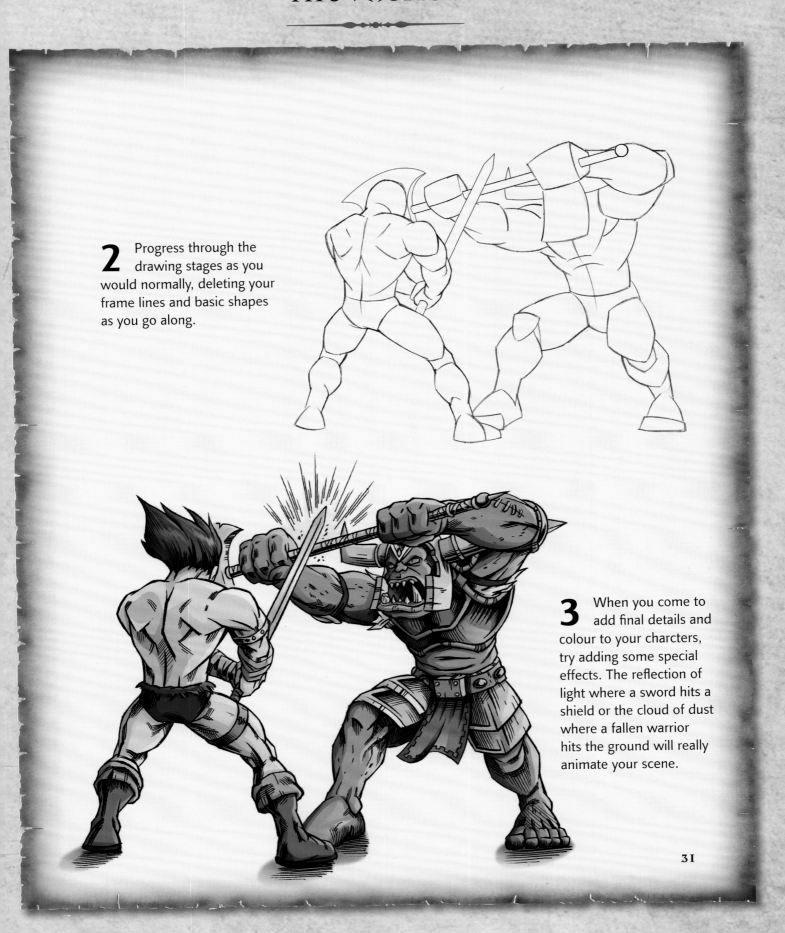

2 Progress through the drawing stages as you would normally, deleting your frame lines and basic shapes as you go along.

3 When you come to add final details and colour to your charcters, try adding some special effects. The reflection of light where a sword hits a shield or the cloud of dust where a fallen warrior hits the ground will really animate your scene.

Glossary

animate bring to life

battlements the top part of a castle wall, with spaces for shooting through

chain mail a kind of armour made from small metal rings linked together

fluid smooth and flowing

foreboding warning of danger

foreground the part of an image nearest to the viewer

furrowed with deep lines or wrinkles

hefty heavy and large

highlights the lightest coloured parts of an image

muted soft and calm

palette the range of colours chosen for a picture

pennants narrow flags

perspective a way of drawing which makes objects look three-dimensional

posture the position of someone's body

texture the way the surface of an object looks or feels

valiant brave and determined

valour courage in battle

vanishing point the place where perspective lines appear to come together into a distant point

Further Reading

Drawing and Painting Fantasy Worlds by Finlay Cowan (Impact Books, 2006)

Fantasy Drawing Workshop by John Howe (Impact Books, 2009)

How to Draw Wizards, Warriors, Orcs and Elves by Steve Beaumont (Arcturus Publishing, 2006)

Index